Rashani brings a rare gift to everything she creates. She is able to celebrate not just the form and the energy but the core of whatever it is she is in relationship with. Equanimity emanates from her prose, her poetry, her artistic renderings and her teachings, as she taps into—then gathers and distills—the key energies of a subject, which in this case is the essence of a prodigious movement. Honoring the diversity, depth, poetry and wisdom of her women friends, colleagues and mentors, Rashani has woven together a tapestry of the Sacred Feminine, beautifully bringing together Her feelings, insights and visions.

—**Dorothy Fadiman**, interculturalist, founder of *Concentric Media*, OSCAR-nominated filmmaker

Rashani Réa's newest book, *A Coven of Dakinis: In Honor of 13 Women Who Have Touched My Life* is mesmerizing. Her artful compositions and the carefully chosen words are a wonderful dance; a definite and clear invitation to fully participate in the celebration of the feminine. Rich in color, shape and texture, each piece is a jewel adorning and framing the immense wisdom available to those who see inside with their whole being.

—**Elena Ascencio-Ibáñez**, meditation and dharma teacher

Rashani is an incessant creative force—uncompromising in vision—an artist of multiple mediums with a voice that comes straight from the soul. Her stunning collages draw you into a journey. There are worlds upon worlds within them. They move you beyond, while also drawing you deeper into your own deep being. Full of circles, they embody the flowing giving and receiving of the energy she names as feminine. There is a peace, wisdom, and possibility in both the artistic beauty of the collages and the words. Each saying is an insight one could spend a lifetime contemplating. The book reflects a contemplation that is also embodied, that is lived in action. Rashani's art and these women's words are also deeply comforting, both naked to suffering and full of hope. In relationship with this book, we can believe in our bones that indeed another world is possible, a world full of wise women and nonbinary imagining where we are all balanced and soaring like the bird.

—**Rev Liza M Neal,** Ministry Beyond Binaries and Borders

With courage and daring that is so needed for the holistic empowerment of future generations, Rashani Réa shatters spiritual boundaries in her newest book, *A Coven of Dakinis.* The patriarchal molds which ensnare contemporary minds are tossed aside by the creation of this powerful dharma artist/dakini, who serves as a testament that spiritual devotion can and should be as dynamic as the womxn in this book. So often we limit ourselves with the false narrative that we must choose a singular path, and that these practices cannot coexist without somehow diminishing their potency. Rashani beautifully challenges these notions and shows the strength of living as an embodiment of a rich spectrum of teachings.

—**Katherine Twomey**, interspiritual, lineage-holding witch

A Coven of Dakinis weaves color, design and wisdom together in an exquisite work of harmony, light and promise. A special offering for this winter solstice 2020.

—**Louise Wisechild**, author of *The Obsidian Mirror*

When we honor the Women
We honor all of Life
Birthers of the cosmos on earth
Rashani distills the profound depths and medicine of these 13 brilliant souls
Into seeds that we can plant into our hearts and the altars of this world
And for the rest of our lives, enjoy the beauty and wisdom that will unfurl from these seeds
Surprising us at times during our daily movements
Gifting us with the perfect medicine that the inner shaman and sage ordered
These seeds have a sacred place in the Akashic Records of this new earth we are birthing

—**Darshan Mendoza**, founder & CEO of 13 Temples, author of *The Luminary Journey*
and the upcoming *13 Temples : An Oracular Blueprint for New Earth Stewardship*

This waka, or canoe you have the privilege of holding and unfolding, is part of the key to our evolution. We are not solving problems, or attacking problems with hammer-like solutions, we are setting off evolutionary waka or pathways that will unfold way beyond all of us. This beautiful offering of Rashani's is part of this movement—she is, we are—and she has brought those that have inspired her and many of us, into something that we can hold and feel this power of a new future they are all pointing at—all these women pointing to a new moon. I stand with you to honor them and you. Bless you for this gift Rashani—so needed.

–**Louise Marra**, systems healer, innovator, depth worker

In this magical, exquisite collage work, I trust you will find a page that comes close to stopping time and mirroring your essence. "By meeting pain with a tender presence, we transform our wounds and losses into fierce grace." My life is described in this sentence! That someone — Rashani — encourages and sees a "tender presence" within me, is such a gift. When I look closely, I see that tender presence touching pain has made for me a life of fierce grace. This lovely book could offer you such a revelation.

–**John Fox**, author of *Poetic Medicine: The Healing Art of Poem-Making*

Rashani Réa brings the wisdom of the *Sacred Feminine* to life with her vibrant collages, an art she has cultivated so beautifully over the 30 years I have had the pleasure of knowing this amazing woman. Her talent for combining truly inspiring quotes with her eye for textures and colors creates *Sacred Art* that graces those who gaze upon them.

–**Katrina Wynne**, counselor, author of *An Introduction to Transformative Tarot Counseling: The High Art of Reading*

Here on Big Island Hawai'i during the defense of Mauna Kea, Auntie Pua taught hula to the people and said, "Dance is a frontline action." This blew my mind. Singing, Dancing, Prayer are frontline actions. Song, poetry, myth, collage, poetic discourse, pulling up roots at the directive of the Great Mother and foraging the disavowed parts of ourselves is a Vow, an action, rooted in the primordial body of Awakening, a craven wish, that in truth is a "collective caravan" promising to altar/alter the Soul of the World, of all Beings everywhere.

Rashani's book title, *A Coven of Dakinis*, and assembly of collages is ignition. Fuel. Initiation, for the dismantling and reorienting of all we know. Here on the land, the space from where this book birthed, all activities are both groundless and groundbreaking—like Rashani, like a dakini.

No one owns the Earth's places of refuge. Just like no one owns a woman's Soul once she has passed through the pages of this initiation. There is an Eloquence of Power arising from the womb tomb Mother as she returns from her thousands of years of descent. Rashani is midwife, songstress, gardener and thief—stealing back the worship of the Sun within the Solar Feminine. Rashani is the voice of creation and destruction and fearless wisdom, HER act of revelation, an uprising unto herself!

–**Alison Fast**, mythic poet/writer, filmmaker and artist in residence, Kipukamaluhia Sanctuary

To open this book is to enter a temple. Each page a portal into a wondrous pool of beauty and wisdom. Rashani's ethereal, exquisite art adds a transportive, transcendent dimension to the already enlightened accompanying texts. Do your beautiful soul a great favor and nourish it deeply with this book.

–**Chelan Harkin**, author of *Susceptible to Light: Poetry by Chelan Harkin*

A Coven of Dakinis

In Honor of Thirteen Women Who Have Touched My Life

Words by Aisha Salem, Arisika Razak, Brooke Medicine Eagle, Dawna Markova,
Dhyani Ywahoo, Estelle Frankel, Jamie K. Reaser, Joanna Macy, Maya Luna,
Mirabai Starr, Ricky Sherover-Marcuse, Ryūmon H. Baldoquín and Tara Brach

Cover design, collages, preface and afterwords by Rashani Réa

Foreword by Dr. Catherine Anraku Hondorp, Sensei

Introduction by Susannah Grover

SACRED SPIRAL PRESS

P.O. Box 916
Na'alehu, Hawai'i
96772

808 929-8043

www.rashani.com

A Coven of Dakinis: In Honor of Thirteen Women Who Have Touched My Life

Cover design, collages, preface and afterwords © Rashani Réa, 2020

Foreword © Dr. Catherine Anraku Hondorp, Sensei 2020

Introduction © Susannah Grovner, 2020

ISBN: 9798574436752

With overflowing love and gratitude this book is dedicated to Joanna Macy,
the "bodacious bodhisattva" who took me in—under her open wing
nearly four decades ago when my pin feathers were still fragile,
moist, and developing ... and showed me, through
her kindness and unwavering example,
how to sharpen the sword
of true compassion

.

.

and with never-ending love,
dedicated also to Dorothy Fadiman
who I have known for the past 55 years.
Dorothy is a continuous inspiration, a true friend
and so much more. Her wisdom lamp shines brightly as she
interweaves the visions and values of people throughout the world.
Thank you for being an awake woman in this ever-changing world, for taking
your vows to clarity and for showing us all how to co-create an anti-nuclear family!

There is a Cherokee prophecy that speaks about this century. It states that the bird of humanity has a male wing and a female wing. The bird of humanity has been flying for centuries with primarily only its male wing and the female wing has been unable to extend. Due to this, the male wing has gotten overly muscularized to the point of violence and the bird of humanity has been soaring in circles—unable to fly in the right direction. The prophecy says that in the 21st century the female wing will fully extend and express itself wholly—in all human beings.

The male energy will relax and the bird of humanity will soar. The feminine, yin, or omega principle has long been cast out or shamed within many societies. However, this is the very essence that our world is needing. It's the exhale, the silent wisdom, the intuition, the connection to our earth, humanity, love and Creator. As women, we have this essence very alive within us. However, we have learned to become more masculine to survive in this over masculinized world. It is more important than ever that we soften into our feminine again. That we learn to trust our own pace, rhythm and ways of creating and being. It's time for us to focus less on achievement and more on connection...

It's time to learn to lead, create, and manifest by following the subtle messages of the body and heart.

—**Global Sisterhood**

FOREWORD

I have never met Rashani Réa. I have no experiences to share with you of Rashani as a person, spiritual guide, teacher, gardener, mother, artist, a wise dharma sister, musician, activist, council and retreat facilitator—or any of the myriad manifestations of Rashani Réa. I cannot speak from the perspective of a longtime friend, nor let you in on how it is to be sitting in her garden with a cup of tea listening to the sounds of the morning in her sanctuary on the Big Island of Hawai'i, home to Pele—though I dream of the time when this might be. So imagine my surprise when I was gifted with the invitation to write the Foreword to her newest book, *A Coven of Dakinis: In Honor of 13 Women Who Have Touched My Life.*

It is exactly because of 'not knowing' Rashani, that I am free to speak unencumbered of the naked impact of her work. With one exception: I have lived with one of Rashani's collages next to my bed for the past sixteen years. In this way her art has deeply touched my life.

The book you now hold in your hands is a sumptuous gallery of collages vibrating in a dance of resonant partnership with turning phrases from each of the individuals she has chosen. Each phrase offers a shift in consciousness guided by Rashani's artwork into a subtle energetic landscape for contemplation.

This latest offering of Rashani's is not one to rush through. To appreciate it fully, you must linger. Find a comfortable seat. Bring awareness to your body. Allow your gaze to take in your surroundings. Place the page in front of you. At first, you may just read the words, admire the beautiful dance of shapes and colors, imagine each womxn* speaking to you. Yet, don't stop there! Release your thinking mind. Soon the page opens, embraces you, breathes you, and takes you deeper. This is where the magic is. Stay for a while and return often. I can assure you, one page can nourish you for a very long time.

In both of the spiritual traditions I embody, the one I was born into—Protestant Christianity—and the one I adopted—Zen Buddhism—one must search wide and deep to find the few stories of womxn who have come before us. *A Coven of Dakinis: In Honor of 13 Women Who Have Touched My Life,* is not only ingenious and inspirational, it is essential and timely. A beautiful book bringing tribute through contemporary voices, voices that root back through the long lineage of womxn's wisdom, wisdom that has been demonized, persecuted, and silenced.

When I first heard Rashani's title, *A Coven of Dakinis,* a spark of excitement rose through my entire body, followed quickly by a catch in my breath; it felt scary to speak of covens. In my body I could still feel the restricting imprint of cellular trauma from centuries of persecution and abuse of women. The twisting and shrinking of internalized fear and underlying shame passed down through all women's maternal lines. A burden still actively carried in my own female body.

Then I remembered PINK PUSSY HATS! The visual impact of a sea of women when we took to the streets, marching, dancing, showing our outrage, and being outrageous, all across this globe, on January 21, 2017, reclaiming the word *'pussy'* by placing its pinkness as a crown on our heads. A worldwide tsunami of pink. *Yes!* My body said, feeling the energy freeing up, riding the power of joy, fearless in our visibility, grounded and supported by millions of beings.

Rashani Réa's book verifies that womxn are still speaking as leaders, sages, witches, teachers, muses, priests, igniting the dakini lineage spark of love, wisdom, courage, and connection for ALL throughout time and space.

A Coven of Dakinis: In Honor of 13 Women Who Have Touched My Life is a perfect title for Rashani Réa's book. As one of Tibet's most renowned dakinis, Machig Labdrön (1055-1153) shows us by her life as example; we too can go to the places that scare us and not be timid…nor fear…taking our rightful seat.

For it is when we join together in sisterhood, in groups, in circles, in marches, in celebration, and yes, in covens, that we summon breaking open the cages of our own enslavement, the closets of our hiding, and embody the courageous sorcery necessary NOW to heal ourselves, each other, and our ailing Mother planet.

–Dr. Catherine Anraku Hondorp, Sensei
Two Streams Zen Sanctuary
Presently on Indigenous lands of the Mohican,
Nipmuc and Pocumtuc peoples
On the Full Moon of November 2020

As a cisgender, queer, white womxn I choose this spelling to create a pause, to wake us up, and to challenge the assumptions of what it is to be in our bodies. To incite questioning the historical use of a term. To make us aware of the power, and the inherent biases, held within the conventional spelling of a word. To honor trans, non-binary, gender queer, and all those that do not fit into conventional gender roles. And, in recognition of the intersectional nature of identity itself.

PREFACE

The word "coven" seems to be a controversial and triggering word for many people. Our conditioned minds are quick to create negative images, associations and opinions of witches and witchcraft—many of which are untrue. For me, the word simply indicates a group of thirteen women.

In ancient times, witches, crones, and hags were often midwives, sages, soothsayers, healers and herbalists, prophets, visionaries, luminaries and leaders who were respected for their wisdom, intuition and sanctity. As the establishment of patriarchy evolved, between 3100 B.C. to 600 B.C., female autonomy gradually disappeared—and the dignity of women slowly eroded. Originally revered as "the crowned ones," elder women became known as 'the crones.' "The holy ones" became known as 'the hags' and "the wise ones" became known as 'the witches.'

The renowned activist, womanist and writer, Alice Walker, wrote the following: "Since the time of the witch burnings, the grandmothers and the healers and the midwives have been systematically targeted. And burned at the stake for hundreds of years, decimating whole communities."

Misogyny flows invisibly in the veins of women and female-identified persons, cross-culturally, manifesting as self-doubt, self-loathing, insecurity and anxiety—and various other forms of internalized oppression, originating from what I perceive as "core deficiency stories"—inherited from our matrilineal ancestors.

Dakani too seems to be a charged word. It has many levels of meaning and the dakini principle can easily be misunderstood. In Sanskrit, a dakini is a female messenger of wisdom and a female embodiment of enlightenment. *All* women are believed to be some kind of dakini expression, appearing in countless forms. Sometimes they incarnate as mentors or messengers and other times as guardians. Dakinis are often playful and elusive, brilliant and intuitive, undeviating, dauntless and radical, imbued with sharpness and clarity.

Tenzin Palmo, a British woman who in 1964 became the second Western woman to be ordained in the Vajrayana Buddhist tradition said, "To me the dakini principle stands for the intuitive force."

Others believe that a dakini is anyone who has cut through deception. In actuality, dakini is simply primordial feminine dynamism/wisdom—named by Hindus and Buddhists—yet it existed l-o-n-g before clockocracy was invented. The definition I most resonate with is expressed beautifully by Ven. Dhyani Ywahoo, the founder and spiritual director of Sunray Meditation Society:

"...It means to be a spark for others, offering pointers or skillful methods through which others can recognize the waves of their thoughts and actions and eventually arrive at the shore free from illusion."

I am using the word **dakini** to define the women whose words of illumination are interwoven with my personal collages throughout this book. There are many women friends and mentors whose words I would have liked to include; many of them appear in my book *Touched by Grace: Through a Temenos of Women*, published in 2016. Those who *do* appear in this particular convergence of poetry, wisdom and wonder, insight and understanding are the ones who responded to my emails in time, as the fire of creativity took its course.

As it turns out, there are *thirteen* women whose words are in these pages. Hence, "A Coven of Dakinis." They are beloved friends, sacred mirrors and mentors—all of whom I have personally interacted with. Each has enriched and blessed my life profoundly, intimately and uniquely.

All of these women are irreplaceable lamps of wisdom, cross-pollinating perennial wisdom. They have been instrumental in midwifing and mirroring facets of my authentic expression — since we are all here/now awakening together as one interdependent, indivisible, intricately braided, Song of the Great Mother.

With the exception of Ricky Sherover-Marcuse, a remarkable woman who spent many years assisting others in "unlearning racism," all of the women are alive. They are all luminescent sparks from diverse traditions, ethnicities and religions—carrying centuries of timeless wisdom. All have known profound loss and suffering and have transformed poison into nectar, pain into medicine—in this amazing time of The Great Turning! Perhaps this title, "A Coven of Dakinis" called out to me because I spent many decades in different Buddhist sanghas, within and outside of eco feminist movements, time with indigenous wisdom keepers in South and

North America, and with Dream Weavers in Aotearoa and Australia—immersed in earth-based spirituality—attempting to accept and find a balance with what seemed like two contrasting aspects of my life: The Wild Woman/Primordial Priestess/Radical Activist and the Zen Roshi/Poised Bodhisattva/Impartial Non-doer. It took me several years to realize that the division I thought was real is simply *imaginary* and that these seemingly different parts are all integrated, fundamental expressions of my unfragmentable wholeness.

I remember a particular morning that profoundly changed my life. In the mid 1980's, I attended a large women's gathering at the Ojai Foundation in southern California and felt fortunate to receive wisdom and direct transmissions from a remarkable group of women gathered by Joan Halifax. Teachers, medicine women, visionaries, mystics, activists, poets, spiritual pioneers and holy rebels.

At the opening of the retreat, we were asked to pray for rain due to a serious drought, which was parching the land. We gathered in a large, circular yurt. Tsultrim Allione, author of *Women of Wisdom*, the groundbreaking book on the lives of great women spiritual practitioners of Tibet, was asked to open the circle with prayers and Buddhist invocations.

Tsultrim entered the yurt in silence, holding in one hand a Tibetan singing bowl and in the other hand a small wooden mallet. After a few poised steps, Tsultrim stopped and gently rang the consecrated bowl. With a soft voice she asked us to pray to the Buddhas and Bodhisattvas, to the numerous Taras, Dakinis and awakened beings—and to the guardian spirits of the land so that the land would be blessed soon with rain. Again, ever so gently, she invited the bowl to sing with a tender tap on its metal rim and took several slow, carefully gaged steps towards the center of the yurt. After placing the bowl mindfully on an altar, she brought her hands together and bowed several times to complete her morning offering. The circle of women was held in deep silence.

A few minutes later Luisah Teish, an Oshun chief and well-known Yoruba priestess, entered the yurt—shamelessly bare breasted and wildly engaged in the moment. She grabbed the Tibetan bowl from the altar and with unrestrained passion began pounding the bowl as if it were a drum. Luisah fervently cried out with demonstrative words: "We've got to *give* our liquid back to the MOTHER! We need to pee on the land! We need to squeeze our breasts and offer our milk to the MOTHER!"

The women in the room were thunderstruck. Both Luisah and Tsultrim were consistently congruent and powerful in their prayers yet polar opposites in their styles. I realized that day that "truth" is unequivocal. By being true to themselves—and to their lineages—they modeled to us a widespread spectrum of feminine love, truth and authenticity. I knew that somewhere within this magnificent continuum was my own authentic expression— 'the song that is my life.'

In 1990, Thich Nhat Hanh invited me to join the The Order of Interbeing. As a form of "engaged Buddhism," it emphasizes the application of Buddhist teachings and compassion to face the injustices and challenges of daily life. I was ordained the following year.

Shortly before taking the 14 precepts, a fiercely compassionate friend and teacher said to me, "Please don't become another dead Buddhist! That brown jacket will become too small for you very quickly. The dharma you carry is v-a-s-t and predates the Buddha Dharma by many thousands of years."

At the time I didn't know what she meant. Now I do.

Year after year, I watched countless women, including myself, acquiesce in the Buddhist sanghas. Those of us who attempted to talk about or question the racism, sexism and homophobia, rampant in many Buddhist communities, were (quietly) reproached. We were accused of disrupting the peace. Like our mothers before us, we went silent—at least for a while.

From the prenatal silence erupted symptoms and dreams—as powerful expressions from the collective Dream Body, in an attempt to reclaim the disavowed and disallowed parts of our wholeness and humanness. In those days, I often recited Audre Lorde's poignant poem to my sangha sisters:

> "Black mother Goddess, salt dragon of chaos, Seboulisa, Mawu.
> Attend me, hold me in your muscular, flowering arms,
> protect me from throwing any part of myself away."

Throughout the 1970's and 80's I brought a small mindfulness bell to many women's music festivals in Europe, Canada, and North America and from 1988 until the mid 90's I brought my guitar, rattles and drums to Plum Village, the center founded by Thich Nhat Hanh (Thay) in France. Thay often invited me to share songs. I opened his dharma talks, in France and throughout the U.S., with soetry (songs and poetry) for many years. In 1992, with Thay's permission and blessings, I organized a Summer Solstice women's ritual in the large zendo at Plum Village. It was a deeply transformative and healing experience for *many* women.

○ ○ ○ ○ ∼ ○ ○ ○ ○

Like most of my books, this one was not "planned." In fact, I had taken a break from collaging due to the hundreds of hours spent creating my last two books. However, early one morning while listening to a stirring dharma talk I felt an unexpected flicker of inspiration. I knew, without knowing, that I was being summoned.

That small 'flicker' awakened into a wildfire! As is customary when seized by the muse, I spent several days incubating in my studio—gathering words, completely surrendered to and guided by the Tao. Unstoppable creativity poured through me for an entire lunation, during which time I designed more than fifty collages. At times I felt as if I was practicing Contact Improvisation—a partner dance form, which emphasizes a shared point of contact and unpredictability. The shared point of contact in *this* dance being the ineffable space in and through which another's words catalyze an image through me from the ineffable silence of silences.

I have no idea how this happens and I'm still as amazed as I was more than fifty years ago when I began collaging. I become immersed in a flowing stream of consciousness, transported by the wonder of its own fluidity. It is a profound self-emptying process. As you will see, the images often morphed from one into the next with subtle changes—and continue to visually echo one another throughout the book.

I honestly think that every book will be the last one. And then, unexpectedly, the Mystery seizes my mind and lovingly hurls me into emptiness, the zone of no-thing, the unknowable source—out of which creativity is birthed, again and again. And inexplicably again.

It seems that we are all being called now—in different ways—to an inner sanctum, free from confusion, beyond doubt and belief, where together we can transform the illusion of separation and the façade of limitation. Toni Packer eloquently reminds me, "Listening silently in quiet wonderment, without knowing anything, there is just one mysteriously palpitating aliveness."

Rashani Réa
Kipukamaluhia Sanctuary
December first, 2020

P.S.

In August of 1982, three months after my mother's death, my seven-year-old son and I boarded a plane for New Delhi, India. I was *not* looking for a teacher. After startling synchronicities and an unexpected encounter with a Tibetan Buddhist nun on the long train ride from New Delhi to Amritsar, we ended up in Dharamsala—a small hillside city on the edge of the Himalayas; home to the Dalai Lama and the Tibetan government-in-exile.

Though I did not think that I was looking for a teacher, a remarkable teacher appeared. A treasured Rinpoche who had recently emerged from eight years in a cave, high in the Himalayas. He took us into his humble home and through his love, generosity and wisdom reminded us, day after day, of the preciousness of life, the priceless endowment of awareness and the unfathomable mystery of existence. He gifted us each with a Tibetan name and mantra, blessed our journey and turned my mind completely inside out!

As we left his home for the last time he whispered, "Remain invisible." Bowing with closed, smiling eyes he said, "No need to shave your head or wear robes. Whoever needs your medicine will find you! One day you will be assisting *many* people—showing them how to untie the knots of ignorance and suffering."

The name he gave me is "Yeshe Khandro." Yeshe in Tibetan means wisdom and Khandro means dakini.

INTRODUCTION

What you are holding in your hands only appears to be a book. Do not be fooled into believing that this is all it is. Of course, you may simply enjoy each wonderful offering at face value, however know that any page has the potential to become its own jumpgate; a portal into another dimension of consciousness or realm of being. Some of the offerings may open for you now, others in another moment.

How can one convey what discovery awaits on the other side of a portal? It is a matter of individual revelation, according to each one's own connection to Source. This is what makes such a book potentially be more than just a book. These authoresses seem to know something about portals they wish to share with you, and there are many portals both known and unknown to humans.

One such portal is called the Kalachakra or the wheel of time. Though from one perspective time is an illusion, it is nevertheless a coordinate we honor, as time is one of the metrics we reference in our world, and on this side of that portal we find ourselves in an extraordinary Cosmic moment. We are currently approaching the Solstice point of our wheel, which will be in three days from this writing, and this Solstice is accompanied by 'The Great Conjunction' of Jupiter and Saturn peaking on the same day in a closeness of proximity and declination such as has not happened for several hundred years.

These two almost opposite-themed planets of expansion and contraction, respectively, will be so close in space that they will appear as one, unified. Meanwhile, today is the day, at least in the Tropical Zodiac, that Saturn enters the sign of Aquarius, which, according to Western Astrology, has profound significance. Add to this another piece of planetary news reported in an article I was reading an hour ago on a science website of a most unusual occurrence on Neptune. It is baffling astronomers. The headline reads, "Dark Vortex on Neptune Changes Direction in Never-Before-Seen Phenomenon."

It seems a dark storm that had been steadily moving towards Neptune's equator has suddenly reversed course and is now moving towards the planet's polar ice caps. Not unlike the times we are in, no one really knows what this means. While reading about Neptune's shift, I was feeling the relief that comes with not knowing, at least a pause in mind activity which can allow a deeper knowing to reach us. At that point a recognition also arose that today is the Urs of the Persian poet Mevlana Jelaluddin Rumi. Urs means the remembrance of the day he died.

In honor of this, there are celebrations of his passing into 'Union with the Beloved' on the 17th of December each year in many parts of the world. This is the time when the Mevlevi Dervishes (named after Mevlana) are performing the ritual of the Sema, turning in absorption—turning away from things known—into union with the Mystery, Itself.

The Sema is happening now as I am writing this, which feels both auspicious and worthy of mention. So I am here, contemplating these concurrent threads emerging: the art of turning, sudden mysterious reversals, the union of planets and dervishes, when a surprising email from Rashani arrives with a request for me to write something for her new book.

I am one who pays attention to synchronous events as they enter my awareness, to see what resonance, or theme, or some guidance may be arriving. I sometimes refer to this as the 'Newspaper of Now.' And now I am writing something for a book whose title is 'A Coven of Dakinis: In Honor of Thirteen Women Who Have Touched My Life.'

First response… what a fascinating title! I feel honored and what comes to mind is my first encounter with Rashani's words almost three decades ago, reading the line, 'There is a brokenness out of which comes the unbroken.'

It portends as a blessing. At the time I was sure the author must have been a Mystic from another era or possibly another dimension. It was years later I learned Rashani is, in fact, a contemporary and we have many friends in common. Since then I have come to deeply respect and appreciate that her expressions implicitly or explicitly point to the reality that manifestation is the un-manifest, that time is timelessness.

We were born for this wondrous moment, as witnesses, participants in a surface world story as it is imploding, dissolving, purifying, perhaps simply realizing itself as awakening from a strange dream of separation—of a once unsustainable way of life, now yielding to an emerging intelligence, wise and unprecedented.

Many seem to be awakening now, recognizing, perhaps for the first time: our home is a feminine planet and she is our Mother, a living emanation of The Mother. Indigenous cultures have known about a time when The Mother reclaims her rightful sovereignty, this theme showing up in many ways now on the world stage and through the collective, in popular culture, at a time when the last hand of an era of patriarchy is playing itself out. She is responding.

As the Native American activist, John Trudell, said, "We were put here on this sacred Mother Earth to serve a purpose… The Earth will take care of us if we will remember the Earth." We are in various stages of remembering now, along with the feminine wisdom she brings.

This is when Dakinis make their presence known, because Dakinis tend to be present for such transition times. And where there are Dakinis, there is magic stirring.

Case in point is but one of the book's offerings, like a masterful turn of a crystal into prismatic splendor: Maya Luna's potent, activating words, 'What you call the apocalypse is my Holy Resurrection.' Get this!

So, yes, it may be our good fortune that *A Coven of Dakinis* has found its way to our hands. The contributors may be the messengers of Dakini invocation. I would encourage you to open the book and let your eyes land lightly on a page; next, to lightly contemplate the space between the words, and then close the book and let the Unknown take you where it will. Maybe sleep next to the book and perhaps its very presence will bring messages to you through your dreaming. Good dreaming! Good awakening!

Thank you, Dakinis. And thank you, Rashani, for what comes into being through your envisioning. May you, readers, receive the blessings of this offering and these times, including realizing yourself as a living blessing.

Thirteen gratitudes, in the flow of this ever-evolving Now,

Susannah Grover
Lauragais, France
17 December 2020

It is
our time, our choice,
to re-energize the fabric
of compassion.

Dhyani Ywahoo

For
all of us,
the starting place
of healing
is reconciliation
with our own
heart...

Tara Brach

Presence
is the portal to
everything we cherish.
And arriving is a "relaxing
back" — a resting
in what is.

Tara Brach

Activism
cannot succeed
when it is fueled
by separation,
aggression,
anger.

Only kindness, love and connection
will bring us true freedom.

Ryūmon H. Baldoquin

Humor and relaxation
are the two primordial qualities of awakenment.

Ryūmon H. Baldoquín

By meeting pain with a tender presence,

we transform our wounds and losses into fierce grace.

Tara Brach

I am the flower that sprouts
From your speechless mouth
What you call the apocalypse is my
Holy Resurrection

Maya Luna

You are made from
Sacred thread
Stretching back
To the beginning
Of time

To the wound
That broke this world
Into existence

Maya Luna

When you sit in silence and turn your gaze
toward the Holy Mystery you once called God,

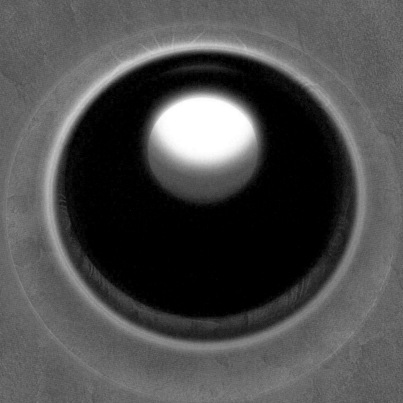

the mystery follows you back out into the world.

Mirabai Starr

In these times of wild unknown, where nothing is solid
and the future is shrouded in dark mystery

We gather to listen
and feel Her pulse

Maya Luna

We must let go
of our sense of injustice
to be effective spiritual
activists.

Ryūmon H. Baldoquin

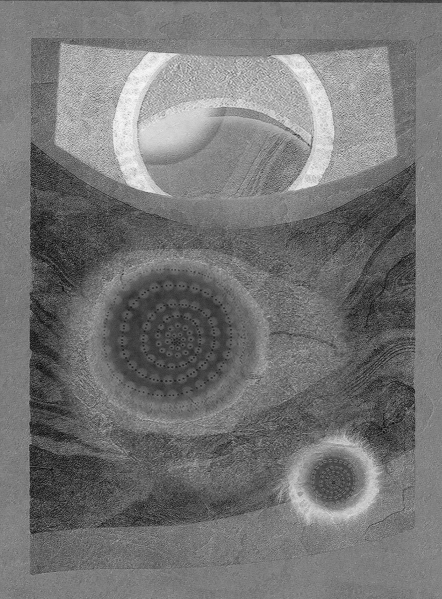

Assume that in spite of the ways we have been divided,
it is possible to reach through these divisions, to listen to each other well
and to change habitual ways of acting which have kept us separated.

Ricky Sherover-Marcuse

Will you grow wide with the wonder
waiting in your heart?

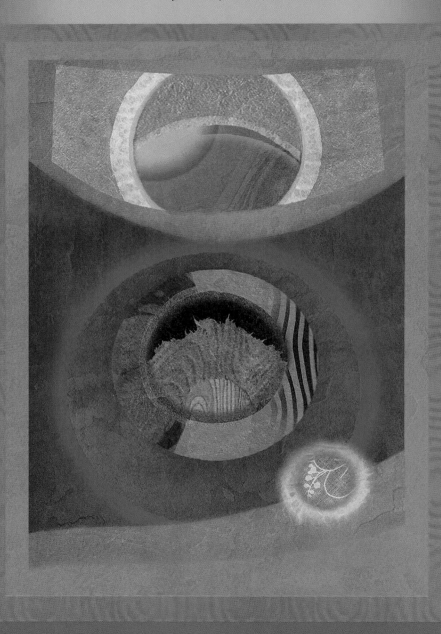

Dawna Markova

Walk
amongst the broken fragments of possibilities
like a rainbow dressed in shadows.

Walk
between the gates of midnight
spinning unimagined bridges with invisible thread.

Walk
to the very edge of this keening world
becoming a benediction within yourself.

Dawna Markova

in a moment like this
when the unknown is lapping at your toes
may you rise in the tide of tears that crests and falls.

Dawna Markova

When the heart awakens,
we remember we are all relatives
in this dance.

Dhyani Ywahoo

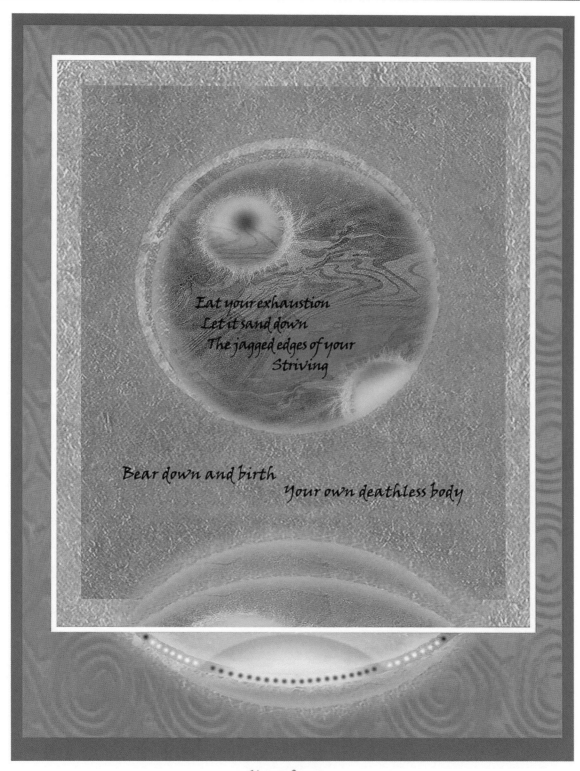

Eat your exhaustion
Let it sand down
The jagged edges of your
Striving

Bear down and birth
Your own deathless body

Maya Luna

WHEN SOMEONE SAYS TO US,
AS THICH NHAT HANH SUGGESTS,
"DARLING, I CARE ABOUT YOUR SUFFERING,"
A DEEP HEALING BEGINS.

TARA BRACH

Words can lead us to grace, and they can
call us away from the inherent sacred.

Jamie K. Reaser

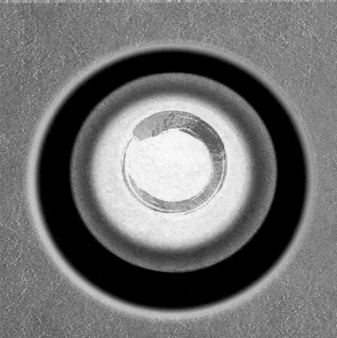

THE DHARMA COMES IN MANY DISGUISES.

RYŪMON H. BALDOQUÍN

The boundary to what we can accept
is the boundary to our freedom.

Tara Brach

The situation is not hopeless;
people can grow and change;
we are not condemned to repeat the past.

Ricky Sherover-Marcuse

Suffering is our call to attention,
our call to investigate
the truth of our beliefs.

Tara Brach

SPIRITUAL WARRIOR'S PLEDGE:

NOT FOR MYSELF ALONE,
BUT THAT ALL THE PEOPLE MAY LIVE.

Brooke Medicine Eagle

We cannot change things as they are...
we can only impact what arises before us

Ryūmon H. Baldoquín

WE ARE HERE
TO WEAVE A WEB OF MERCY.

ARISIKA RAZAK

每一刻

LISTEN

RECEIVE

HEAR WHAT YOU KNEW

LONG BEFORE YOU KNEW

YOU KNEW

MAYA LUNA

It's that knife-edge of uncertainty
where we come alive to our truest power.

Joanna Macy

Freedom
requires the ability

to embrace uncertainty—
to not know what is going to happen next,
and to trust in life's unfolding journey
moment by moment.

Estelle Frankel

Hope is a verb.

Joanna Macy

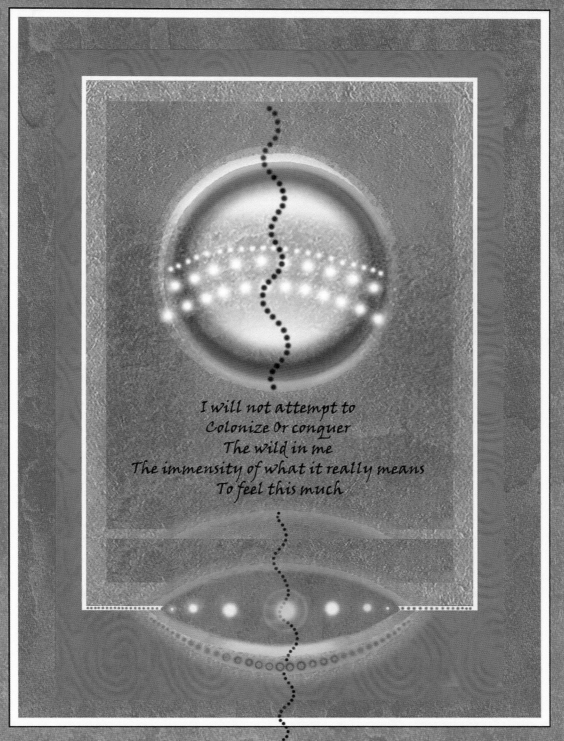

I will not attempt to
Colonize Or conquer
The wild in me
The immensity of what it really means
To feel this much

Maya Luna

COMPASSION IS THE MAGNETISM
THROUGH WHICH POTENTIALS
ARE EXPRESSED.

Dhyani Ywahoo

We're seldom schooled to hold life in respect,
to enlarge our ability to love,
take care of, and be respectfully
connected with all things around us.

Brooke Medicine Eagle

ASSUME
THAT YOU ARE
THE EXPERT OF YOUR
OWN EXPERIENCE

AND THAT YOU HAVE INFORMATION
WHICH OTHER PEOPLE NEED TO HEAR.

RICKY SHEROVER–MARCUSE

PERCEIVE ALL CONFLICT AS PATTERNS OF ENERGY
SEEKING HARMONIOUS BALANCE AS ELEMENTS IN A WHOLE.

Dhyani Ywahoo

and internalized oppression that prevents them

Assume that it is only other people's own oppression

(temporarily) from being effective allies to you at all times.

Ricky Sherover-Marcuse

Grace happens
when we act with others
on behalf of our world.

Joanna Macy

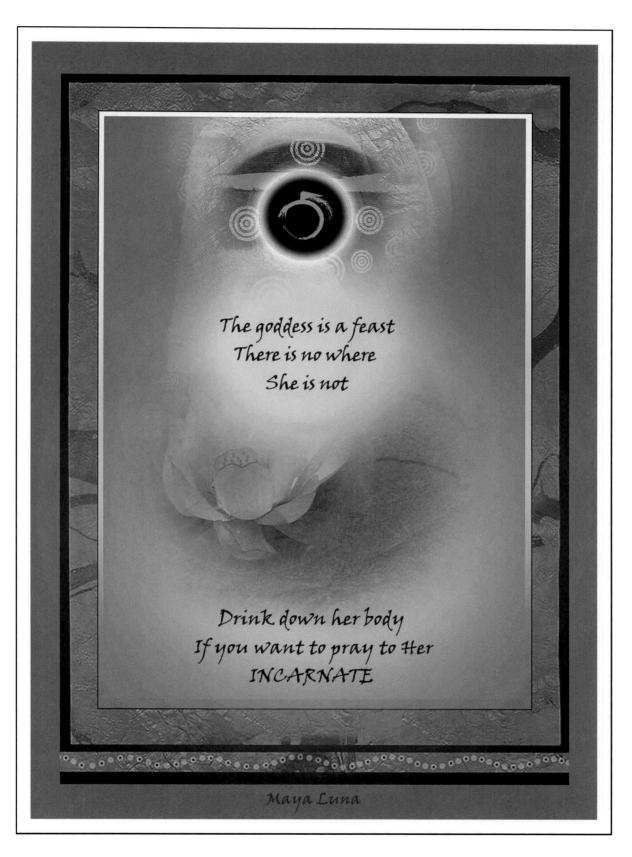

The goddess is a feast
There is no where
She is not

Drink down her body
If you want to pray to Her
INCARNATE

Maya Luna

The human mind and heart are unfathomable, infinite mysteries.
Wisdom emerges in the space between knowing and not knowing,
discovery and mystery, action and stillness, words and silence.

Estelle Frankel

Do what calls your heart;
effective action comes from love.

It is unstoppable and it is enough.

Joanna Macy

In the face of impermanence and death,
it takes courage to love the things of this world

and to believe that praising them is our noblest calling.

Joanna Macy

This is what it is like when heaven and earth
conspire to turn time into something else,
something still waiting for words to describe it.

Jamie K. Reaser

Look inside.
Follow the compass
of night.

Aisha Salem

Our way ahead
must be based on true inspiration.
On That which cannot be predicted,
caught or anything but deeply
surrendered to—in our
humility to be real
—from moment
to moment.

Aisha Salem

The Mother,
She, definitely is Coming
to devour our separate sense of self
through passionate liberation.

Aisha Salem

We would much rather be undefined
than ordained in traditions that don't fit our curves.

Mirabai Starr

People
of all faiths
call her Mother.

In moments of deeply personal sorrow,
we turn to her for consolation.
In our bewilderment,
we turn to her for insight.

Mirabai Starr

Mother of suffering,
you carry the grief of the whole world
in your boundless, shattered heart.
Please, carry mine.
I know that the broken-open container
of your Mother's Heart
has room for us all.

Mirabai Starr

Any of us can dream,
but seeking vision is always done
not only to heal and fulfill one's own potential,
but also to learn to use that potential
to serve all our relations...

Brooke Medicine Eagle

There is containment and there is flow.
Without flow, containment is rigidity.
Without containment, flow is chaos.

Ryūmon H. Baldoquin

Gratitude, respect and honor
to all of life.

Arisika Razak

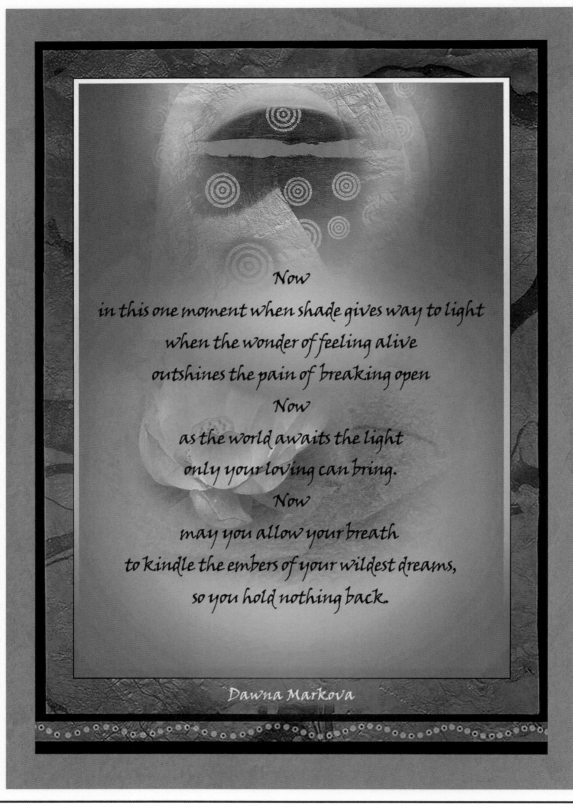

Now
in this one moment when shade gives way to light
when the wonder of feeling alive
outshines the pain of breaking open
Now
as the world awaits the light
only your loving can bring.
Now

may you allow your breath
to kindle the embers of your wildest dreams,
so you hold nothing back.

Dawna Markova

WE ARE NOT HERE TO WORK.
WE ARE HERE
TO DANCE AWAKE THE SACRED DREAM.

Brooke Medicine Eagle

We
do not need to be afraid
of the emptiness.

It is in
boundlessness that we meet the Real
and recognize it as the face of Love.
It is in groundlessness that we find
our way home.

Mirabai Starr

Fundamentally,
EMBODIMENT
MATTERS.

ARISIKA RAZAK

Embrace your attachments
Submit to your unholy entangled
Earthly desires
These are the swords that cut you
Deep
These are the knives that cut you
Open
That piece you so the medicine
Flows in
The sacred ache of your wanting
Is the only force strong enough
To break
You
Down

Down to the foundation
Where you are ash to the flame
Where you are total and utter defeat
This is the secret altar of Love
Adorned with the roses of bittersweet
Fulfillment
Adorned with the skulls of naked truth
Filled with the smoke of disillusioned dreams
This is the secret altar of love
This is rock bottom
Where at last true freedom can arise
When in doubt....
Follow the Ache

Maya Luna

Other books by Rashani include:

Beyond Brokenness
 (The Danish version is called *Sangen I Sorgen*)
The Time of Transformation is Here
Chakra Poems
A Soft Imminence of Rain: Celtic Poems by Alice O. Howell
A Cry of Windbells
My Bird Has Come Home
The Unfurling of an Artist: Early Collages and Calligraphy of Rashani Réa
Welcome to the Feast: In Celebration of Wholeness
Is The Bowl Empty or Is It Filled with Moonlight?: Turning Words and Bodhi Leaves
Mahalo: Visual Koans for the Pathless Journey
Always Choose Love
Moonlight on a Night Moth's Wing: A Fusion of Image and Word
True Golden Sand
Timeless Offerings
The Way Moonlight Touches
Shimmering Birthless: A Confluence of Verse and Image
An Unfolding of Love
Touched by Grace: Through a Temenos of Women
Territory of Wonder
Gossamer Mirrors
In Praise of Love: A Dialogue Between a Dove and a Ladybug
The Disappearance
The Threshold Between Loss and Revelation
A Brief Collision with Clockocracy
I Can Hear Her Breathing
Collaborating with the Inevitable
The Fire of Darkness: What Burned Me Away Completely, I Became
Only One Surrender
Three Children's Stories, which include: *Present Moment, Colorful Moment: Sharing Present Moment Awareness with Children, Tao and the Moon* and *Can You Draw a Shooting Star?: A Child's Experience and Expression of Loss*
The Mercurial Impermanence of Aliveness
Who or What Remains?
Pencil Sharpeners and Thunderstorms
Rashani also created collections of collages for *Leaves from Moon Mountain* by Dorothy Hunt and *Gathering Silence* by Ivan M. Granger

AFTERWORDS

Tomorrow is the Solstice and the great conjunction of Jupiter and Saturn. In the Northern Hemisphere seeds of Collective Dreaming, long labyrinthed, are breaking open with/in the holy darkness. And in the Southern Hemisphere the longest day of the year will be celebrated. Tomorrow I will be doing the *final* layout of these pages so that the book will be officially birthed on this auspicious day. The process of co-creating *A Coven of Dakinis* has been unlike any other book. The title alone has disturbed, delighted, aroused, angered and awakened others. A close friend exclaimed, "The title of this book is revelatory, Rashani. It immediately reveals to the reader how quickly their mind creates images, beliefs, constructs and stories."

A friend of a friend said that she could not write an endorsement for the book because the title, for her, felt like cultural appropriation. I sat for many days with her feedback, allowing it to open and swallow me. Her perspective invited me to drop into a deeper space of naked, compassionate inquiry—a graceful plunge for which I am profoundly grateful. Accusations of cultural appropriation have become a common occurrence over the past several years—and rightly so. A question I find useful, which I shared in a group last weekend as a dyad exercise is, "Through what filters do you perceive reality?"

I reached out to many friends—asking if the title, for them, had ANY trace of cultural appropriation. If it had, I was ready to change the title to "A Coven of Wisdom." Being respectful of, a fierce ally with, and sensitive to, marginalized people—having been put in this category myself—I would not want in any way to offend or disrespect anyone from a less dominant culture.

As for the word "coven," which has also shaken up several people, a friend who I deeply respect exclaimed, "This is an important word here! It symbolizes a powerful reclamation for *all* women, Rashani—just as the word "queer" has been, and is, for lesbian, gay, bisexual, and transgender people."

A relative of a friend who interacts primarily with people in their thirties said, "They need Rashani's book desperately but would not open it if the words "dakini" or "coven" were in the title. Another friend remarked that the foreword is "too radical." And another friend believes that the introduction detracts from the book. Oh, la la! This feels like a microcosm of our entire planet. For me, everyone's voice is an essential part of the whole song. I welcome all of the diverse expressions of the Beginingless Source.

One of the thirteen women responded with, "I am pro Dakini. And I love this title but wow it has stirred up a lot hasn't it!? ... You're a witch and a dakini and these are your friends... so, it makes sense to me! We are your coven of Dakinis." Another of the thirteen women replied, "I'm fine with your title and trust the beauty and spirit that you are bringing to this." And another replied, "Honored to be part of the coven."

Other friends' responses:

"Rashani, the cover is wonderful and the title, *A Coven of Dakinis*, is to me more awakening and original than *A Coven of Wisdom*, which may seem much safer, but is not as cracking in its healing flames."

"I read your mail and I know exactly where you drew the name from when it presented itself. I wouldn't give it anymore thought. The person who sees cultural appropriation is being kind and considerate but coming from a mind of "being cautious" rather than moving on God's Dance & Play. I choose to come from the latter and respect/trust the play of words as I Get them, to serve exactly what they're meant to. If someone gets triggered, frankly speaking, don't they need to be? Anyone knowing anything of you will know the total harmlessness and love in it. I trust your surrender a helluva lot more than I trust cultural political correctness."

"I love the title and what you've written. It feels important to speak up now when so many people seem to be running in their limbic systems, not their cognitive thinking brains. To shock, even disorient, with mere words—that's powerful—and then to dispel the fears and open people up to mystery and magic!"

As empaths and women, we care so much, sometimes too much, about being correct and not harming others. This 'title dance' moved from flowing and staccato, through chaos and lyrical, into stillness and has been a valuable blesson (blessing and lesson) in quietly refusing to compromise my inner knowing and direction. To trust the inner re-membering that I'm simply an infinitesimal particle in this 'one mysteriously palpitating aliveness' being activated by the collective field for a greater awakening.

Rashani Réa
12 . 20 . 2020

As of fifteen minutes ago, The Hawaiian Volcano Observatory has detected a new Kīlauea eruption happening inside Halemaʻumaʻu crater. Tūtū Pele has reappeared. How amazing!

SHOULD YOU WISH TO DISCOVER MORE
ABOUT THESE WONDERFUL WOMEN:

Aisha Salem: https://aishasalem.com

Arisika Razac: https://www.ciis.edu/faculty-and-staff-directory/arisika-razak

Brooke medicine Eagle: https://www.medicineeagle.com

Catherine Anraku Hondorp: www.twostreamszen.org *and* www.networkspinal.com

Dawna Markova: https://www.dawnamarkova.com

Dhyani Ywahoo: https://sunray.org/oversight/

Dorothy Fadiman: https://www.concentric.org

Estelle Frankel: http://estellefrankel.com

Jamie K. Reaser: http://hiraethpress.com/jamie-k-reaser/

Joanna Macy: https://www.joannamacy.net

Maya Luna: https://deepfemininemysteryschool.com/maya-luna

Mirabai Starr: https://www.mirabaistarr.com

Ricky Sherover-Marcuse: https://www.marcuse.org/herbert/people/ricky/ricky.htm

Ryūmon H. Baldoquín: www.twostreamszen.org

Susannah Grover: https://www.facebook.com/theineffablestream

Tara Brach: https://www.tarabrach.com

Printed in Great Britain
by Amazon